Michigan

Souvenir Journal

Adventure Publications
Cambridge, Minnesota

Introduction

From the hubbub of downtown Detroit to the wild shoreline of Isle Royale, Michigan has something for everyone. This book contains 60 of the best tourist sites in the state, and it's perfect to use as a keepsake after a visit, thanks to the handy space allotted for jotting down notes. You can also use it as a guide to help you find a new site to explore. The book includes everything from shipwrecks and lighthouses to fine arts, sports, and, of course, the inner workings of the Motor City's famous automobile factories. If you can, try to visit them all, and along the way, have fun and enjoy this souvenir guide to Michigan.

Edited by Sandy Livoti and Brett Ortler
Cover and book design by Jonathan Norberg

Front cover photo: Mosquito Beach at Pictured Rocks National Lakeshore by Mark Stacey, Michigan Weather Service Forecast Office (see page 128 for complete photo credit)

Back cover photos: Top left, Ford Piquette Avenue Plant third floor by Stephen Brown; sjb4photos on flickr.com; bottom right, Eastern Market by Eastern Market Corporation; Point Iroquois Lighthouse; Tulip Time Festival by Rachel Kramer.

Photo credits:
Grayling Visitors Bureau, page 4; Huron-Manistee National Forest, page 5; Genesee County Parks and Recreation Commission, page 10 and 11; Eastern Market Corporation, page 18 and 19; Charles H. Wright Museum of African American History, page 20; Stephen Brown; sjb4photos on flickr.com, page 22 and 23; Deb Nystrom, page 25; Angela Loyd, A Healthier Michigan/Blue Cross Blue Shield of Michigan, page 27; © Steven G. de Polo 2015, page 29; © Detroit Institute of Arts, USA / Bridgeman Images, page 30 and 31; Rick McOmber, page 33;

Photo credits continued on page 128

10 9 8 7 6 5 4 3 2 1

Copyright 2016 by AdventureKEEN
Published by Adventure Publications
820 Cleveland Street South
Cambridge, Minnesota 55008
(800) 678-7006
www.adventurepublications.net
All rights reserved
Printed in the U.S.A.
ISBN: 978-1-59193-566-7; eISBN: 978-1-59193-607-7

Table of Contents

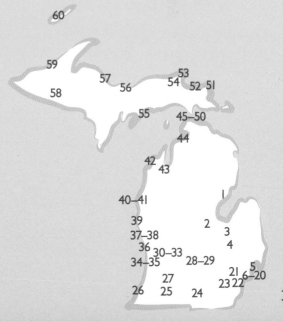

Lumberman's Monument and Hartwick Pines State Park

OSCODA, MICHIGAN

Lumberman's Monument is a 14-foot memorial overlooking the Au Sable River. Here you can experience what it was like to be a lumberjack in the 1800s. You can climb through a logjam, learn how to use a crosscut saw or hike to the *wanigan* (floating cook shack). In addition to the hands-on fun, the site also features exhibits, demonstrations and videos.

One of the largest state parks in the Lower Peninsula, Hartwick Pines covers over 9,650 acres. Rich in scenery and history, it has nearly 50 acres of old-growth pines. The pines stand as reminders of Michigan's important past in the lumber industry, which is also chronicled at the park's fascinating Logging Museum.

Date visited

Notes

ERECTED TO PERPETUATE THE MEMORY OF THE
PIONEER LUMBERMEN OF MICHIGAN THROUGH
WHOSE LABORS WAS MADE POSSIBLE THE
DEVELOPMENT OF THE PRAIRIE STATES

Dow Gardens

MIDLAND, MICHIGAN

When you need peace and quiet, the Dow Gardens are the perfect destination. With 110 acres to see, you can explore the grounds at your leisure or just pick a spot and relax. The site offers golf cart tours, as well as tours of the garden and the stately, historic Dow family home, which is affectionately known as "The Pines."

Admission to Dow Gardens includes entry into nearby Whiting Forest, where you can walk the paths through 2½ miles of plants and ponds in the midst of the city. During your excursion, you'll also see a 30-foot lookout tower and a charming covered bridge.

Date visited _____

Notes _____

_____

_____

_____

_____

Zehnder's Holz Brücke Covered Bridge

FRANKENMUTH, MICHIGAN

There's nothing quainter and more romantic than a covered bridge. German for "wood bridge," the Holz Brücke spans nearly 240 feet as it crosses the Cass River near Frankenmuth. It was the dream-come-true for Eddie and Tiny Zehnder, brothers who envisioned a nineteenth-century covered bridge to complement their nearby Bavarian-style restaurant and hotel complex. The bridge was constructed on land and pulled over the water by an oxen team laden with pulley-like equipment. It took 12 days to place it! Dedicated in 1980, it accommodates hundreds of thousands of vehicles and pedestrians annually.

Date visited _____

Notes _____

_____

_____

_____

_____

Crossroads Village and Huckleberry Railroad

FLINT, MICHIGAN

Things are much simpler at Crossroads Village. This authentic, turn-of-the-last-century town has a community of folks ready to welcome you to several dozen historic structures. At Crossroads, you can explore a blacksmith shop, the opera house, a general store, a carriage barn, a cider mill and other vintage destinations. If you want to learn a historical trade, such as toy- or broom-making, you can do it here.

A 40-minute ride on the Huckleberry Railroad can add more thrills. The authentic Baldwin steam locomotive will take you along the shores of Mott Lake to the historic Pere Marquette roadbed, and then back to the village.

Date visited _____

Notes _____

_____

_____

_____

Edsel and Eleanor Ford House

GROSSE POINTE SHORES, MICHIGAN

As you might expect given their last name, Edsel and Eleanor Ford had a passion for automobiles, but they also were deeply interested in architecture, art, gardening and nature. The family's magnificent 87-acre estate and their historic mansion are a testament to all of these interests. Visitors can view their diverse collections of art, antiques and furniture, which reveal the family's progressive tastes in design. Estate tours both inside and outside the residence are available, as are guided bird walks. December is a popular month to visit because the beautiful grounds are even more spectacular with thousands of lights glimmering during the annual Winter Wonderland event.

Date visited _____

Notes _____

_____

_____

_____

_____

Comerica Park

DETROIT, MICHIGAN

The official ballpark of the Detroit Tigers, Comerica Park can host up to 40,000 cheering fans, and there's a good deal more to be seen here than just the view from your seats. There's a "liquid fireworks" fountain in center field, where the water sprays change color to the beat of music. In the main concourse, you can browse sports displays and photos dating back to the 1800s. While you're out strolling, you'll see statues of the greatest Tigers players and the beautiful hand-painted tigers on the park's famous carousel. When the ball club isn't in town, Comerica also plays host to many concerts and other events.

Date visited _____

Notes _____

_____

_____

_____

_____

Guardian Building

DETROIT, MICHIGAN

The Guardian Building is a 40-floor marvel of classic art deco architecture, complete with vaulted ceilings, imported marble and granite, Monel metalwork and even a doorman. A prime business center, the Guardian also features specialty shops and restaurants in its picturesque promenade. Best of all, its vantage point downtown offers spectacular panoramic views of Detroit and Windsor.

Date visited

Notes

Eastern Market

DETROIT, MICHIGAN

The Eastern Market is the largest and oldest outdoor farmers market in the United States. Covering more than 4½ acres, it has 100-plus shops and cafes. Paths lead to tempting arrays of fresh vegetables, fruits, meats and specialty foods, as well as floral and art offerings. There's also music and other entertainment; if that's not enough, you can join a walking tour to learn about the area's colorful history, which includes long brewing traditions and tales of rum-running. The holidays are an especially good time to visit, as the market has nearly everything you can think of when it comes to gifts, trimmings, treats and trees.

Date visited _____

Notes _____

_____

_____

_____

_____

Charles H. Wright Museum of African American History

DETROIT, MICHIGAN

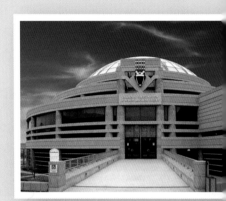

African American history is American history! For a cultural experience you won't forget, visit the famous and beautiful Wright Museum. It's the largest institution in the world dedicated to African American art, history, heritage and achievement, and it is a must-see for all ages and races. The Ford Freedom Rotunda, featuring a 65-foot-high glass dome, is astonishing by itself. The museum has many profoundly inspiring collections and artifacts, and the special galleries about Harriet Tubman, the Underground Railroad and Detroit's labor movement are not to be missed. For mementos of your visit, African American and African art, collectibles and books are available at the museum store.

Date visited _____

Notes _____

_____

_____

_____

Ford Piquette Avenue Plant

DETROIT, MICHIGAN

Rev up your road trip with a stop at the birthplace of the Model T. Most people don't know that this revolutionary car was first developed and built in a three-story mill. Now protected as a historic site on both the state and federal level, the building is one of the world's most significant automotive heritage sites and the oldest auto factory worldwide that gives public tours. Here, you'll walk the same plank floors that were worn down by the construction of 12,000 Model Ts. Tour guides will lead you through the assembly exhibit, the experimental room, collections of rare Detroit-built cars, Henry Ford's office (which was re-created as it looked in 1908) and much more.

Date visited _____

Notes _____

_____

_____

_____

_____

Anna Scripps Whitcomb Conservatory and Belle Isle Park

DETROIT, MICHIGAN

At Anna Scripps Whitcomb Conservatory, novices and master gardeners alike will be awestruck by the vast collection of orchids and the myriad other plants found here. The Scripps' setting on historic Belle Isle also provides easy access to Belle Isle Park and its nearly 1,000 acres. The crown jewel of Detroit's public park system, Belle Isle offers everything from a golf course and a children's zoo to a maritime museum and an aquarium. It also boasts 150 wooded acres, lakes, picnic areas and amazing skyline views! There's so much to see and do in this area, you'll want to plan your visit ahead of time.

Date visited _____

Notes _____

_____

_____

_____

Detroit Riverfront and Detroit RiverWalk

DETROIT, MICHIGAN

Come out to the shores of the Detroit River to experience the green space of the Riverfront and the RiverWalk. There's enough entertainment on-site to suit everyone; the list includes live music, water shows, riverboat tours, children's activities and more. Traversing the strip is the Dequindre Cut, a recreational greenway that features separate lanes for foot traffic and bicycles. It's also handy because it's a ready connection to the shops, restaurants and other places of interest between the eastern Riverfront and the Eastern Market, just a mile and a half away.

Date visited _____

Notes _____

_____

_____

_____

_____

Ford Field

DETROIT, MICHIGAN

The home of the Detroit Lions, Ford Field seats 65,000 and boasts the best sight lines of any football stadium in the United States. At this 25-acre site, you can enjoy professional sports, as well as concerts, banquets, trade shows and much more. The complex offers upscale food and private lounges, with restaurants and concessions on the ground level. To top it off, the seven-story atrium features a glass wall that provides great views of the city skyline.

Date visited _____

Notes _____

_____

_____

_____

Detroit Institute of Arts

DETROIT, MICHIGAN

It doesn't matter if you prefer contemporary, modern or graphic art because you can find it all at the Detroit Institute of Arts. A Detroit landmark, the museum features more than 100 galleries. Famous American and European artworks are featured, but you can also see other important collections from Africa and Asia, as well as ancient art objects. There's even more to see and do here: Its Friday Night Live! features concerts, magic shows, children's entertainment, films, special exhibits and art workshops. All in all, there's enough at the D.I.A. to make you want to visit again and again.

Date visited _____

Notes _____

_____

_____

_____

Detroit Zoo

ROYAL OAK, MICHIGAN

Everybody has a whole lot of fun at the zoo! From clever chimps and toothy crocs to massive grizzly bears, there are hundreds of species to see. The zoo's main exhibits include the Asian Forest, African Forest, African Grasslands, American Grasslands, Australian Outback Adventure, Arctic Ring of Life, Penguinarium and the Butterfly Garden. And you don't just have to watch the critters; at the Giraffe Encounter, you can actually feed the giraffes from your hand!

Date visited _____

Notes _____

_____

_____

_____

_____

Fox Theatre

DETROIT, MICHIGAN

From the moment you walk through the door, the Fox Theatre transports you back to the wild heights of the Roaring Twenties. Built in 1928, this theater's extravagance is unparalleled: The lobby alone is six stories tall and half a block wide, and its marquee towers an improbable 10 stories tall. The show doesn't stop once you're inside, as the theater's ornate Egyptian, Indian and Asian motifs are as vibrant and intricate as when they were first made. The Fox is also still a premier entertainment venue, and it plays host to everything from Broadway shows like *Beauty and the Beast* to renowned musical groups, entertainers and stand-up comics. So visit the Fox for the vintage architectural spectacle, and stay for its many modern entertainment options.

Date visited

Notes

GM Renaissance Center and Detroit People Mover System

DETROIT, MICHIGAN

The world headquarters of General Motors is a complex of seven interconnected skyscrapers, and it's almost a city unto itself. Here you will find GM vehicles, plenty of shopping, sophisticated dining and a high-rise hotel. Free one-hour tours outline the shared history of GM, Detroit and the Riverfront. You're sure to enjoy the spectacular view from the center tower; there you can see downtown Detroit, the Detroit River, and Windsor, Ontario, just across the river. Once your visit is through, the Renaissance Center's Detroit People Mover System is available to connect you with all the attractions in downtown Detroit.

Date visited _____

Notes _____

_____

_____

_____

_____

37

Hitsville U.S.A. Motown Museum

DETROIT, MICHIGAN

Hitsville U.S.A. is among Michigan's most popular tourist destinations. Founded in 1985, the museum tells the stories of Motown stars who rose from obscurity to worldwide acclaim. You'll experience Studio A and the Control Room, where original equipment and instruments from 1959 to 1972 still grace the rooms. The museum has an extensive exhibition of photos, artifacts and memorabilia, including the sequined gowns and highly styled, matching outfits of the musical groups. It's the perfect place for family reunions, church gatherings and group get-togethers, offering something for musicians, singers, entrepreneurs, history buffs and, of course, the fans.

Date visited _____

Notes _____

_____

_____

_____

_____

Joe Louis Arena

DETROIT, MICHIGAN

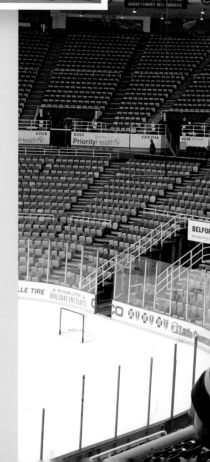

Joe Louis Arena is the home of the 11-time Stanley Cup champion Detroit Red Wings. Located on the banks of the Detroit River, it opened its doors in 1979, and since then it has hosted professional, college and youth hockey, as well as circuses, concerts, ice shows and other thrill-filled attractions. You might find yourself wondering why there's a large octopus sculpture outside the stadium. Red Wings fans often toss octopi onto the ice as good-luck charms because the creatures symbolize the eight wins that used to be necessary to take home the Stanley Cup.

Date visited _____

Notes _____

_____

_____

_____

Mariners' Church of Detroit

DETROIT, MICHIGAN

Mariners' Church of Detroit is the oldest stone church in Michigan. Built in 1842, it served as a critical link in the Underground Railroad. Slaves traveling up from the South made their escape to freedom through a tunnel from the church to the Detroit River, where boats awaited to take them to Canada. The church is also well known for its deep connection to the sailors and the maritime industry. For many years, the church held a service for the lost sailors of the *Edmund Fitzgerald*, chiming its bell 29 times for the 29 souls who perished, as the ballad by Gordon Lightfoot famously recalls. Today, its memorial service commemorates lost sailors from all over the Great Lakes and from the U.S. military.

Date visited

Notes

PEACE · BE · STILL

WHOSE ARM HATH
BOUND THE RESTLES
WAVE

EAR US WHEN
E CRY TO THEE

Holocaust Memorial Center

FARMINGTON HILLS, MICHIGAN

The Holocaust Memorial Center at the Zekelman Family Campus has been teaching about the Holocaust for over 25 years. Its stunning exhibits, programs and the architecture itself have received international recognition. Your heart will stir when you see the artifacts, memorabilia and 3-D reconstructions at the exhibits. In addition, you can hear powerful personal testimonies and attend inspiring conference events and workshops. The library archive will be another eye-opener. Books, recorded oral histories and audio/visual documentaries provide a wealth of facts about the concentration camps. There are genealogical resources for tracing survivors, records of courageous acts, and the annals of the events leading up to WWII.

Date visited

Notes

The Henry Ford and Greenfield Village

DEARBORN, MICHIGAN

You'll never find yourself short of entertaining options at The Henry Ford and Greenfield Village. The Village is divided into seven historic districts. At one, you can see old-fashioned steam locomotives; at another, you can see a painstaking re-creation of Thomas Edison's original laboratory. At the Henry Ford, you can tour the Rouge Factory, which has been producing vehicles since 1921 and makes F-150s today. In addition to the factory tour, the Henry Ford has an IMAX theater, a research center featuring many artifacts, one-of-a-kind restaurants and specialty souvenir stores to top off your day.

Date visited _____

Notes _____

_____

_____

_____

_____

U-M's Matthaei Botanical Gardens and Nichols Arboretum, and the Big House

ANN ARBOR, MICHIGAN

Whether you're a nature lover or a football fan, there's always something amazing happening at the University of Michigan! Gardeners and flower lovers will enjoy the Matthaei Botanical Gardens and Nichols Arboretum and its 700 acres of gardens, greenhouses and natural preserves. Sports fans can catch a game at the historic Michigan Stadium, more commonly called the Big House. The home of Michigan Wolverines college football, it seats over 100,000 fans and is often packed to the brim with maize and blue on game day.

Date visited _____

Notes _____

_____

_____

_____

_____

Michigan International Speedway

BROOKLYN, MICHIGAN

NASCAR's fastest track, the Michigan International Speedway opened in 1968 and quickly became a fan favorite. Seating up to 72,000 today, NASCAR fans often refer to it as the "Great Escape" because it serves as a getaway that both fans and drivers enjoy. With grounds that cover a verdant 1,400 acres, it's not hard to understand why. And thanks to the incredibly fast 2-mile track—where speeds average a whopping 200 miles per hour—the races are a thrilling sensory experience. For a closer look, the speedway also offers behind-the-scenes tours and special events for children and adults alike.

Date visited

Notes

Kalamazoo Air Zoo

PORTAGE, MICHIGAN

For thrill seekers, history and aviation buffs, and kids of all ages, nothing beats the excitement of the Air Zoo! For three consecutive years, it's been voted the "Best Place to Spend a Day with Your Family" and the "Best Place to Take Out-of-Towners." A celebration of air and space flight, it's home to more than 50 historic aircraft, as well as full-motion flight simulators. The Air Zoo also houses a bounty of historical exhibits, hand-painted murals, fine art and even amusement park-style rides.

Date visited _____

Notes _____

_____

_____

_____

_____

Silver Beach Carousel

ST. JOSEPH, MICHIGAN

Thrilling crowds since 1910, the Silver Beach Carousel features hand-carved, hand-painted figures that delight visitors of all ages. In all, it includes 48 creatures, from horses and tigers to clownfish and sea serpents. Once the organ music is over and your ride is complete, there's more to explore. Michigan's tallest kaleidoscope and the Curious Kids' Museum are both nearby; on warm days, it feels great to cool off at the Whirlpool Compass Fountain.

Date visited _____

Notes _____

_____

_____

_____

_____

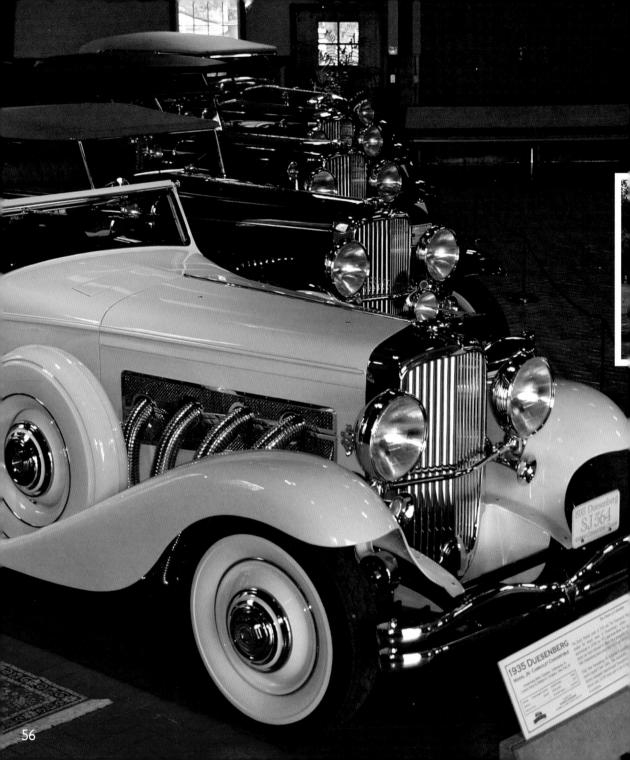

1935 DUESENBERG
Model JN, Cabriolet Convertible

Gilmore Car Museum

HICKORY CORNERS, MICHIGAN

At the 90-acre Gilmore Car Museum, automotive history comes alive! The site has more than 300 classic cars and vintage motorcycles—including everything from the Ford Model A to Duesenbergs, Cadillacs, Studebakers and Chevrolets. Special exhibits of hot rods and bygone brands, like the Hudson, should not be overlooked. The iconic automotive mascots exhibit, which was featured on PBS's "Antiques Roadshow," is on display here as well. The 1930s Shell Service Station is the perfect spot to take photos; and before you leave, you can stop for a bite at George & Sally's 1941 Blue Moon Diner.

Date visited _____

Notes _____

_____

_____

_____

_____

Michigan State University

EAST LANSING, MICHIGAN

If you love sports, you can't miss Michigan State University. One of the storied schools in college athletic history, its teams consistently lure top talent and win big at the 70,000-capacity Spartan stadium. The 300-member Spartan Marching Band, one of the oldest and most celebrated university marching bands in the nation, adds to the entertainment. If you're not interested in sports, the campus itself is well worth a visit, as it's full of interesting places to appreciate, including the Beal Botanical Gardens, the Sanford Natural Area, the planetarium and the art center.

Date visited _____

Notes _____

_____

_____

_____

_____

Michigan State Capitol

LANSING, MICHIGAN

Dedicated to the citizens of Michigan in 1879, the Michigan State Capitol took six years to construct. The stunning Victorian-era building is remarkably ornate; it actually includes more than 9 acres of hand-painted surfaces! If you visit, head to the magnificent rotunda on the fourth floor, as it provides a stunning view. Tours of the public areas are offered and include visits to the Senate and House galleries. Engaging tour guides provide both contemporary and historical information about the building and the legislative process.

Date visited

Notes

Meyer May House

GRAND RAPIDS, MICHIGAN

The Meyer May House was Frank Lloyd Wright's first major commission in Michigan. Completed in 1909, the home was purchased in 1985 and restored. The two-year restoration removed a 1922 addition, rebuilt the roof, replaced ceilings, repaired over 100 art glass windows and skylights, restored a George Niedecken mural and reproduced interior pieces, furnishings and the original landscaping. Once restored, the home opened to the public in 1987, giving visitors the opportunity to experience an original Prairie-style house just as Wright had intended.

Date visited _____

Notes _____

_____

_____

_____

_____

Grand Rapids Public Museum

GRAND RAPIDS, MICHIGAN

The Grand Rapids Public Museum is the second-largest museum in Michigan, and its collections are seemingly endless, ranging from fossils and zoological specimens to antique cars. The collections also include hundreds of thousands of photos, documents and other resources of interest to artists, genealogists, historians, collectors, and scientists. The museum features exhibitions that kids will enjoy and educational programs and special events, to boot! While Wurlitzer organ concerts will inspire some, the Chaffee Planetarium allows others to explore the mysteries of our universe while reclining in comfort.

Date visited

Notes

65

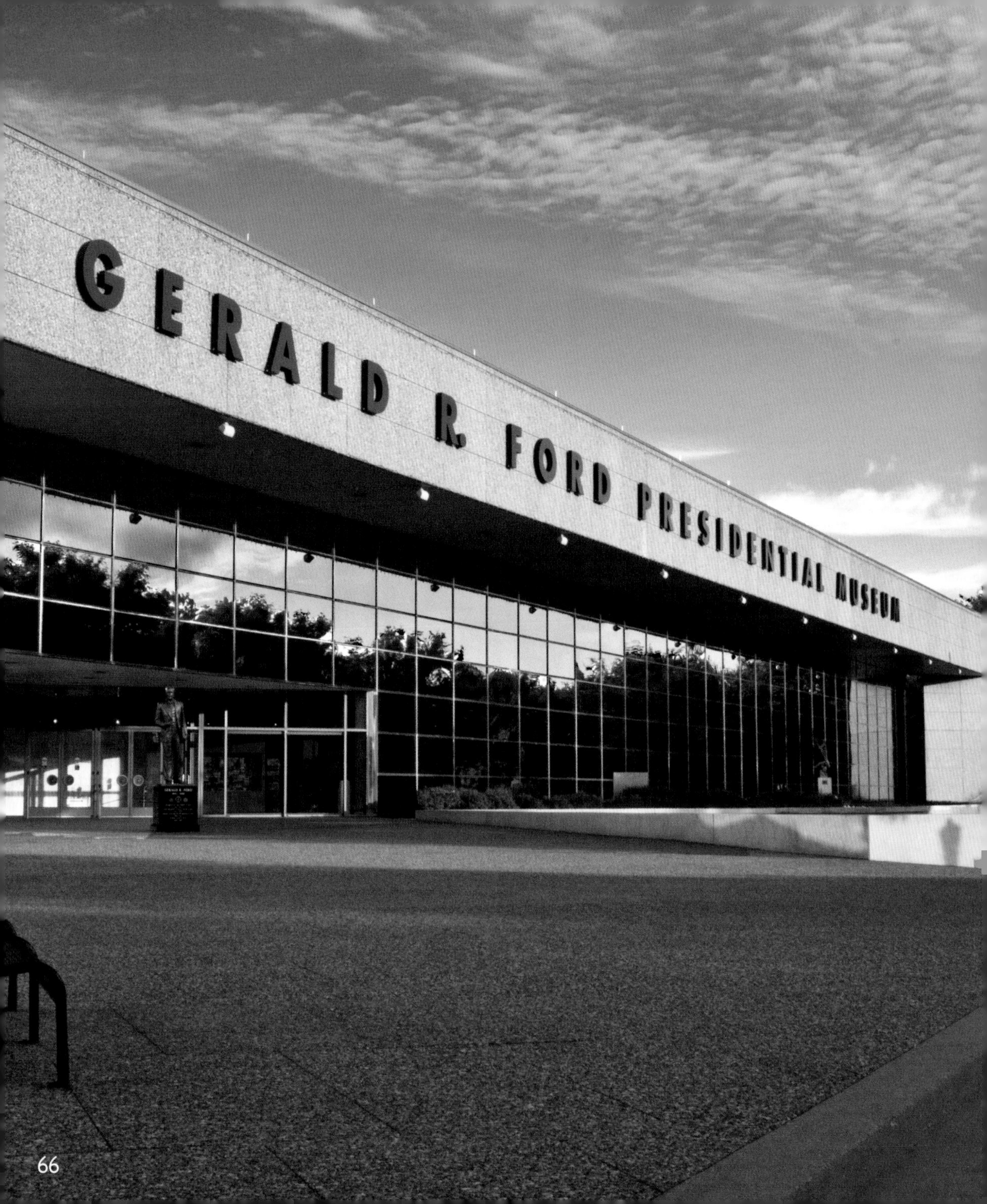
GERALD R. FORD PRESIDENTIAL MUSEUM

Gerald R. Ford
Presidential Museum

GRAND RAPIDS, MICHIGAN

Honoring our nation's 38th president, the Gerald R. Ford Presidential Museum recently underwent a major redesign, adding the 8,000-square-foot DeVos Learning Center, which allows teachers to bring entire classrooms to the museum to study and learn about the political process. The museum also features many historical artifacts from Ford's time in office, and there's even more to see in the digital collections and online exhibits. The Ford Museum also hosts community festivities, naturalization ceremonies and other special events that make a visit even more interesting and educational.

Date visited

Notes

67

Frederik Meijer Gardens and Sculpture Park

GRAND RAPIDS, MICHIGAN

Frederik Meijer's indoor horticulture, outdoor landscaping and world-famous sculptures are sure to inspire you! One of the better known cultural destinations in the Midwest, the site has a lot to offer. The indoor/outdoor gardens also include Michigan's largest tropical bird conservatory, nature trails and a boardwalk. The permanent collection of sculptures is composed of almost 300 internationally acclaimed works, from the likes of artists such as Edgar Degas to Auguste Rodin. While some pieces are displayed in the gardens, you'll find the greatest concentration in the 30-acre Sculpture Park.

Date visited _____

Notes _____

_____

_____

_____

_____

Windmill Island Gardens and Tulip Time Festival

HOLLAND, MICHIGAN

Since 1929, the town of Holland has been celebrating its Dutch heritage. At Windmill Island Gardens, an expanse of 36 acres is graced with 115,000 magnificent tulips. The site also features a 250-year-old, 125-foot-high Dutch windmill, an antique Dutch carousel, canals, dikes and picnic areas. In early May, the famous Tulip Time Festival features Dutch food, Dutch dances, parades with locals in Dutch costumes, concerts and other entertainment. Perhaps best of all, more than 4 million tulips decorate a 6-mile drive through the town's historic neighborhoods.

Date visited _____

Notes _____

_____

_____

_____

_____

Holland State Park Beach

HOLLAND, MICHIGAN

The sunsets over Lake Michigan are reason enough to visit the beach at Holland State Park. This large, sandy beach near the historic Big Red Lighthouse is a great spot to swim, play beach volleyball, windsurf, sail or fish. Other popular pastimes include walking the dunes, strolling the boardwalk, watching shorebirds from the pier or just relaxing and sunbathing. Whatever you choose, there's not much better than a day at Holland State Park's beach.

Date visited _____

Notes _____

_____

_____

_____

Grand Haven Lighthouse

GRAND HAVEN, MICHIGAN

The Grand Haven Lighthouse does more than guide Lake Michigan's sailors. A majestic treasure, it's the place to come for beauty, inspiration and reflection. Located where the Grand River enters Lake Michigan, the lighthouse provides great views of the lake and the channel. Informative signs about its history are set along the pier, and local residents often fish at the dock for salmon. At sunset, photographers flock here to take photos in all seasons.

Date visited _____

Notes _____

_____

_____

_____

_____

Pere Marquette Park

MUSKEGON, MICHIGAN

Pere Marquette Park is a first-rate city park of almost 30 acres. It has a clean, sandy beach on the Muskegon Channel and a variety of amenities, including playgrounds, sand volleyball courts, bike trails and more. The park is also quite close to something a little different: a World War II-era submarine, the *USS Silversides*. A major tourist attraction year-round, the sub sunk many enemy vessels. It now serves as its own maritime museum and is open for tours. Great photo ops of the *Silversides*, the beach and picturesque sunsets over Lake Michigan abound.

Date visited

Notes

Michigan's Adventure

MUSKEGON, MICHIGAN

Michigan's Adventure is the state's largest amusement park and water park. If you're craving speed and thrills, Shivering Timbers, Thunderhawk and Wolverine Wildcat are the park's fastest roller coasters. Children love the Big Dipper and Zack's Zoomer, both delivering roller coaster thrills at slower speeds. Rides like the Grand Carousel, Timbertown Railway and Giant Gondola Wheel are great for family fun, while Elephants, Airplanes, Jr Go-Karts and Motorcycles will delight the littler ones. If it's a water park you're after, WildWater Adventure has three wave pools and more than 20 waterslides.

Date visited

Notes

Silver Lake Sand Dunes and Little Sable Point Lighthouse

MEARS, MICHIGAN

Not far from Lake Michigan is Silver Lake Sand Dunes. Spanning 690 acres, its western shoreline gives way to massive sand dunes that are a draw for all sorts, from hikers, mountain bikers and off-roading thrill seekers to families who just want to relax and make sand sculptures or enjoy the panoramic views of Silver Lake and Lake Michigan.

Historic Little Sable Point Lighthouse is another wonderful place to visit. At an impressive 100 feet tall, this late nineteenth-century lighthouse still uses its original Fresnel lens, which allows the light to shine out to 19 miles. Better yet, you can take a tour and see the view from the top for yourself!

Date visited

Notes

Ludington State Park with Big Sable Point Lighthouse

LUDINGTON, MICHIGAN

The most popular state park in Michigan, Ludington State Park covers 5,300 acres of forest, lakeshore and sand dunes. In addition to its scenic views and nearly 20 miles of marked trails, the park is also home to Big Sable Point Lighthouse. At 112 feet, it's one of the tallest lighthouses in the state. After its construction in 1867, mariners sailing Lake Michigan could see the lamp from 19 miles away! You can climb Big Sable's 130 steps to see stunning views, take a tour or purchase a keepsake at the original Keeper's Quarters, which is now a gift shop.

Date visited _____

Notes _____

_____

_____

_____

_____

S.S. Badger

LUDINGTON, MICHIGAN

The *S.S. Badger* is a national treasure. A true rarity— a coal-fired steamship—it's a link to earlier times. Launched in 1952, the ship carries more passengers per year than any other ship on the Great Lakes, and it's also the largest car ferry to sail Lake Michigan. Its 60-mile cruise takes people and vehicles across Lake Michigan for the three-hour trip between Ludington and Manitowoc, Wisconsin. The *Badger* is more than just a car ferry; it features private staterooms, two lounges, outside deck areas that are perfect for sunbathing and a buffet-style dining area. Kids will be drawn to the video arcade and the playroom, and the pet-friendly vessel welcomes pets aboard too.

Date visited

Notes

Sleeping Bear Dunes National Lakeshore

EMPIRE, MICHIGAN

The dunes at Sleeping Bear Dunes National Lakeshore tower up to 450 feet above Lake Michigan, and the site protects an incredible 35 miles of pristine beaches. Climbing the otherworldly dunes is always a popular activity, but the site is also home to an island lighthouse, a historic logging village, and quaint farmsteads representing the late 1800s to early 1900s. You can also raft, tube, canoe or kayak down the Platte River or go for a hike or a bike ride on the park's 100-plus miles of trails. No matter your interest, Sleeping Bear has got you covered.

Date visited

Notes

National Cherry Festival

TRAVERSE CITY, MICHIGAN

The National Cherry Festival is more than just a single celebration during the summer—it features over 150 events and activities, and most are free for all ages. Family attractions range from parades, air shows, arts and crafts fairs and food events to kid-friendly fun, such as cherry pit-spitting and pie-eating contests, turtle racing and more. You can also visit one of the area's many cherry farms—Traverse City is the Cherry Capital of the World for a reason—and even pick your own cherries to enjoy.

Date visited

Notes

Petoskey State Park

BOYNE CITY, MICHIGAN

Petoskey State Park is a great place to find Michigan's state stone—the Petoskey Stone. A fossilized coral, unpolished Petoskey Stones look a bit like they are covered in a honeycomb pattern, but when they are polished, the stones are a breathtaking look at Michigan's ancient life. To find them, head to the beaches at Petoskey State Park where collecting is allowed (but ask park staff about collecting limits/rules when you visit). The park also includes sand dunes, hiking trails and a pair of modern campgrounds—more than enough reason to make your rockhounding expedition a weekend trip.

Date visited _____

Notes _____

_____

_____

_____

_____

Mackinac Island Ferries

ST. IGNACE/MACKINAW CITY, MICHIGAN

If you want a closer look at the Great Lakes, a ferry trip is a great option. Three ferries operate between Mackinaw City, St. Ignace and Mackinac Island. All of them provide scenic views of the Mackinac Bridge and the Straits of Mackinac. The Star Line Hydro-Jet Ferry features open-air observation decks, enclosed cabins and an engine that produces something of a show— a 35-foot "rooster tail" spray of water in its wake. Shepler's Mackinac Island Ferry offers a main deck lounge with wide aisles, cushioned seats and outside top-deck seating. Arnold Mackinac Island Ferry is the oldest but most modern passenger ferry; the company has been in operation for an incredible 125 years.

Date visited _____

Notes _____

_____

_____

_____

Colonial Michilimackinac

MACKINAW CITY, MICHIGAN

Once a British outpost on the far reaches of the frontier, today Colonial Michilimackinac is located in America's heartland in Mackinaw City. It features a reconstructed fort and fur-trading village, where you can see over a dozen eighteenth-century buildings, replete with period furnishings, themed exhibits and artifacts. It also hosts reenactments and demonstrations that will thrill the kids, including costumed historical interpreters firing muskets and cannons.

Date visited

Notes

95

Grand Hotel

MACKINAC ISLAND, MICHIGAN

A Michigan landmark, the Grand Hotel welcomes guests to Mackinac Island, a decidedly old-fashioned locale where motorized vehicles are prohibited. The island's many horse-drawn carriages and bicycles complement the building's charming ambiance. Built in 1887, the hotel's architecture and elegance are on full display, and its 660-foot front porch (the longest in the world) provides guests with tremendous views of the Straits of Mackinac from the comfort of rocking chairs.

Date visited _____

Notes _____

_____

_____

_____

_____

Mackinac Island State Park and Fort Mackinac

MACKINAC ISLAND, MICHIGAN

Michigan's first state park, Mackinac Island State Park, was established in 1895, and it's chock-full of historic landmarks, stunning views and amazing rock formations. It also has over 70 miles of roads and nature trails—some paved, some not. As cars aren't allowed on the island, sites are accessible by foot, bike, horse, buggy, sightseeing carriage or horse-drawn taxi. The park is also home to Fort Mackinac, which features costumed interpreters, tours and demonstrations at the fort's more than two dozen restored buildings.

Date visited _____

Notes _____

_____

_____

_____

Mackinac Bridge

ST. IGNACE, MICHIGAN

An absolutely striking sight, the Mackinac Bridge connects the Upper and Lower Peninsulas over the Straits of Mackinac, with Lake Huron to the east and Lake Michigan to the west. Spanning 26,372 feet, it's the longest suspension bridge in the Western Hemisphere and the fifth longest worldwide. A trip across the toll bridge will set you back $4 per car, but it's worth it; the road is about 200 feet above the water, providing unobstructed sight lines from your car for miles. Pedestrian traffic on the bridge is banned for safety reasons, but once a year the bridge hosts an annual bridge walk when pedestrians can stroll the 5 miles from St. Ignace to Mackinac City along with tens of thousands of others.

Date visited _____

Notes _____

_____

_____

_____

Castle Rock

ST. IGNACE, MICHIGAN

Once known as "Pontiac's Lookout" by the Ojibwa, Castle Rock is one of the oldest lookout points near St. Ignace. Open for touring since 1929, this natural attraction reaches a height of nearly 200 feet and offers great views of Lake Huron and Mackinac Island. Binoculars are installed at the summit, and you can also see statues of Paul Bunyan and Babe, the Blue Ox, or take a quick jaunt to the gift shop. American Indians fashioned the shop's birchbark ceiling and handcrafted the walls in the 1950s.

Date visited _____

Notes _____

_____

_____

_____

_____

Soo Locks

SAULT STE. MARIE, MICHIGAN

An interconnected system of locks, canals and waterways links the Atlantic Ocean and all five Great Lakes; the Soo Locks are an essential part of this system, enabling freighters, tugboats and other vessels to travel between the lower Great Lakes and Lake Superior. Today, an incredible 5,000 vessels pass through the Soo Locks annually, and ship watching is a popular pastime at the site's observation platform and at Soo Locks Park. If you want a closer look, take a boat tour with one of the tour companies at the Locks and you'll get to see the Soo from the water.

Date visited

Notes

Point Iroquois Lighthouse

BRIMLEY, MICHIGAN

Point Iroquois Lighthouse helped safeguard mariners for nearly 100 years. Retired in the 1960s after an automated beacon was installed farther from shore, the lighthouse was placed on the National Register of Historic Places in 1975. The 65-foot tower and its outbuildings have since been completely restored, and the site now welcomes visitors in summer and winter. On a visit, you can climb the 72-step staircase and see the Canadian shoreline in the distance and freighters sailing to and from the Soo Locks. The site also features tours of the historic keeper's house, and rockhounds will enjoy agate hunting and rock collecting on the beach below.

Date visited _____

Notes _____

_____

_____

_____

_____

Great Lakes Shipwreck Museum

PARADISE, MICHIGAN

The Great Lakes Shipwreck Historical Society first started exploring shipwrecks in Lake Superior in the late 1970s and now operates the Great Lakes Shipwreck Museum. One of the best small museums in the nation, it features many artifacts and exhibits, and people visit from all over the country to see the 200-pound bronze bell that was recovered from the shipwreck of the *Edmund Fitzgerald.* If you're in the market for maritime prints, nautical gifts, lighthouse collectibles or books, the museum's store features a plethora of merchandise pertaining to the ships and shipping on the Great Lakes.

Date visited

Notes

WHITEFISH POINT
LIGHT STATION
1849

Tahquamenon Falls

PARADISE, MICHIGAN

Tahquamenon Falls is one of the largest waterfalls east of the Mississippi. At 50 feet high and over 200 feet wide, the Upper Falls are breathtaking, and they're all the more remarkable for being situated in Tahquamenon Falls State Park and its pristine 52,000 acres. While not as dramatic as the Upper Falls, the Lower Falls are also worth seeing, as there are five smaller falls in all. (Note: The Upper Falls are handicap-accessible, but the Lower Falls are not.)

In addition to the falls, the park has 40-plus miles of hiking trails, boat rentals, a campground, a restaurant, a brewery and more.

Date visited _____

Notes _____

_____

_____

_____

Palms Book State Park

MANISTIQUE, MICHIGAN

Palms Book is where you'll find Michigan's largest freshwater spring, known as *Kitch-iti-kipi,* Ojibwe for "big cold water." This remarkable natural attraction is 200 feet wide and 40 feet deep. Approximately 10,000 gallons of water flow into the spring each minute, and visitors enjoy climbing aboard the observation platform to peer at the trout below. Perhaps the best part is that you can pull the floating observation platform (which is attached by a cable) across the surface of the spring, enabling you to literally go at your own pace.

Date visited _____

Notes _____

_____

_____

_____

_____

Pictured Rocks National Lakeshore

MUNISING, MICHIGAN

One of the most picturesque locations in the country, Pictured Rocks National Lakeshore covers 42 miles of Lake Superior shoreline, and it features sparkling beaches, vibrantly colored sandstone cliffs and awe-inspiring sea caves. All of these draws combine to make Pictured Rocks a photographer's dream. Summertime visitors also enjoy boat cruises, lighthouse tours, birding and diving. In the winter, cross-country skiing, snowmobiling and ice fishing are popular options, making the park a true all-seasons destination.

Date visited _____

Notes _____

_____

_____

_____

Sugarloaf Mountain

MARQUETTE, MICHIGAN

Sugarloaf Mountain is one of the most popular scenic overlooks on Michigan's Upper Peninsula. Its stunning panoramic view of Lake Superior and the surrounding area makes it a must-see when you visit Marquette. There are two options to reach the peak: an "easy" trail via many steps or a "hard" trail where you'll essentially be hiking up the mountain. The summit is home to three observation platforms, each with a view worth seeing. For more great scenery, nearby Indianhead Mountain Resort, Big Powderhorn Mountain Resort and Copper Peak all have much to offer.

Date visited _____

Notes _____

_____

_____

_____

_____

Ottawa National Forest

IRONWOOD, MICHIGAN

Spanning nearly a million acres in the far western portion of the Upper Peninsula, Ottawa National Forest is an outdoor recreation hotspot, as it's home to excellent fishing, camping, and sightseeing. Potawatomi Falls are one popular destination, as is the National North Country Scenic Trail; in all, there are 118 miles of the 4,600-mile trail within the Ottawa National Forest's boundaries.

Date visited _____

Notes _____

_____

_____

_____

Porcupine Mountains Wilderness State Park

CARP LAKE TOWNSHIP, MICHIGAN

At 60,000 acres, Porcupine Mountains is one of the few expansive tracts of wilderness left in the Midwest and Michigan's only state-designated wilderness. The park's virgin pine and hemlock, secluded lakes, miles of rivers and streams, and its more than 90 waterfalls make backpacking through the "Porkies" a fantastic experience! The highest point is Summit Peak, with an elevation of over 1,950 feet. On a clear day, the 40-foot observation tower provides a splendid view of the park and surrounding areas. Other attractions include the beautiful Presque Isle River and the incomparable Lake of the Clouds.

Date visited _____

Notes _____

_____

_____

_____

_____

Isle Royale National Park

HOUGHTON TOWNSHIP, MICHIGAN

Isle Royale National Park is the largest wilderness area in the state. Consisting of 450 islands that surround Isle Royale itself—the park preserves more than 132,000 acres. Because it's situated in Lake Superior, the park is only accessible by ferry, seaplane or personal watercraft. Even though it's secluded, the park has a lot to offer—from backcountry hikes and scenic vistas to offshore shipwrecks and the always wild weather of Lake Superior. Whether you're a nature lover, a backpacker, a boater or a diver looking for a remote adventure, this park is the one to explore.

Date visited _____

Notes _____

_____

_____

_____

NAME	PAGE	SITE INFORMATION
Anna Scripps Whitcomb Conservatory and Belle Isle Park	24	Inselruhe and Conservatory Avenues, Belle Isle, Detroit, MI 48207; 313-331-7760; www.belleisleconservancy.org 2 Inselruhe Avenue, Detroit, MI 48207; 844-235-5375; www.michigan.gov/dnr
Castle Rock	102	N2690 Castle Rock Road, St. Ignace, MI 49781; 906-643-8268; www.castlerockmi.com
Charles H. Wright Museum of African American History	20	315 Warren Avenue East, Detroit, MI 48201; 313-494-5800; www.thewright.org
Colonial Michilimackinac	94	102 Straits Avenue West, Mackinaw City, MI 49701; 906-847-3328; www.mackinacparks.com
Comerica Park	14	2100 Woodward Avenue, Detroit, MI 48201; 313-962-4000; www.detroit.tigers.mlb.com
Crossroads Village and Huckleberry Railroad	10	6140 Bray Road, Flint, MI 48505; 800-648-7275; www.geneseecountyparks.org
Detroit Institute of Arts	30	5200 Woodward Avenue, Detroit, MI 48202; 313-833-7900; www.dia.org
Detroit Riverfront and Detroit RiverWalk	26	www.detroitriverfront.org
Detroit Zoo	32	8450 10 Mile Road West, Royal Oak, MI 48067; 248-541-5717; www.detroitzoo.org
Dow Gardens	6	1809 Eastman Avenue, Midland, MI 48640; 800-362-4874; www.dowgardens.org
Eastern Market	18	2934 Russell Street, Detroit, MI 48207; 313-833-9300; www.easternmarket.com
Edsel and Eleanor Ford House	12	1100 Lake Shore Road, Grosse Pointe Shores, MI 48236; 313-884-4222; www.fordhouse.org
Ford Field	28	2000 Brush Street, Detroit, MI 48226; 313-262-2000; www.detroitlions.com
Ford Piquette Avenue Plant	22	461 Piquette Street, Detroit, MI 48202; 313-872-8759; www.fordpiquetteavenueplant.org
Fox Theatre	34	2211 Woodward Avenue, Detroit, MI 48201; 313-471-3200; www.foxtheatredetroit.net
Frederik Meijer Gardens and Sculpture Park	68	1000 East Beltline Avenue Northeast, Grand Rapids, MI 49525; 888-957-1580; www.meijergardens.org

Gerald R. Ford Presidential Museum	66	303 Pearl Street Northwest, Grand Rapids, MI 49504; 616-254-0400; www.fordlibrarymuseum.gov
Gilmore Car Museum	56	6865 Hickory Road West, Hickory Corners, MI 49060; 269-671-5089; www.gilmorecarmuseum.org
GM Renaissance Center and Detroit People Mover System	36	400 Renaissance Center, Suite 2500, Detroit, MI 48243; 313-567-3126; www.gmrencen.com People Mover: www.thepeoplemover.com
Grand Haven Lighthouse	74	Grand Haven State Park, 1001 Harbor Avenue, Grand Haven, MI 49417; www.lighthousefriends.com
Grand Hotel	96	286 Grand Avenue, Mackinac Island, MI 49757; 800-334-7263; www.grandhotel.com
Grand Rapids Public Museum	64	272 Pearl Street Northwest, Grand Rapids, MI 49504; 616-929-1700; www.grpm.org
Great Lakes Shipwreck Museum	108	18335 Whitefish Point Road North, Paradise, MI 49768; 888-492-3747; www.shipwreckmuseum.com
Guardian Building	16	500 Griswold Street, Detroit, MI 48226; 313-963-4567; www.historicdetroit.org
Hitsville U.S.A. Motown Museum	38	2648 Grand Boulevard West, Detroit, MI 48208; 313-875-2264; www.motownmuseum.org
Holland State Park Beach	72	2215 Ottawa Beach Road, Holland MI, 49424; 616-399-9390; www.michigan.gov/dnr
Holocaust Memorial Center	44	28123 Orchard Lake Road, Farmington Hills, MI 48334; 248-553-2400; www.holocaustcenter.org
Isle Royale National Park	122	www.nps.gov/isro/index.htm
Joe Louis Arena	40	19 Steve Yzerman Drive, Detroit, MI 48226; 313-471-7000; www.olympiaentertainment.com
Kalamazoo Air Zoo	52	6151 Portage Road, Portage, MI 49002; 269-382-6555; www.airzoo.org
Ludington State Park with Big Sable Point Lighthouse	82	8800 M-116, Ludington, MI 49431; 231-843-2423; www.visitludingtonstatepark.com
Lumberman's Monument and Hartwick Pines State Park	4	5401 Monument Road, Oscoda, MI 48750; 989-362-8961; www.fs.fed.us 4216 Ranger Road, Grayling, MI 49738; 989-348-7068; www.michigan.gov/dnr
Mackinac Bridge	100	www.mackinacbridge.org

Mackinac Island Ferries	92	Arnold Mackinac Island Ferry: 800-542-8528; www.arnoldline.com Shepler's Mackinac Island Ferry: 556 Central East; Mackinaw City, MI 49701; 800-828-6157; www.mackinacisland.net/sheplers Star Line Mackinac Island Ferry: 587 State Street North, St. Ignace, MI 49781; 800-638-9892; www.mackinacisland.net/starline
Mackinac Island State Park and Fort Mackinac	98	Fort Mackinac: 7127 Huron Road, Mackinac Island, MI 49757; State Park: 7165 Main Street, Mackinac Island, MI 49757; 906-847-3328; www.mackinacparks.com
Mariners' Church of Detroit	42	170 Jefferson Avenue East, Detroit, MI 48226; 313-259-2206; www.marinerschurchofdetroit.org
Meyer May House	62	450 Madison Avenue Southeast, Grand Rapids, MI 49503; 616-246-4821; www.meyermayhouse.steelcase.com
Michigan International Speedway	50	12626 U.S. Highway 12, Brooklyn, MI 49230; 517-592-6666; www.mispeedway.com
Michigan State Capitol	60	Capitol Avenue at Michigan Avenue, Lansing, MI 48933; 517-373-2353; www.capitol.michigan.gov
Michigan State University	58	220 Trowbridge Road, East Lansing, MI 48824; 517-355-1855; www.msu.edu
Michigan's Adventure	78	1198 Riley-Thompson Road West, Muskegon MI 49445; 231-766-3377; www.miadventure.com
National Cherry Festival	88	250 Front Street East, Suite 301, Traverse City, MI 49684; 800-968-3380; www.cherryfestival.org
Ottawa National Forest	118	Covering much of the western portion of Michigan's Upper Peninsula; 906-932-1330; www.fs.usda.gov/ottawa/
Palms Book State Park	112	LAT 46.004772000000003 LONG -86.385047, Manistique MI, 49854; 906-341-2355; www.michigan.gov/dnr
Pere Marquette Park	76	Beach Street and Lakeshore Drive (Bluffton) – 3510 Channel Drive, Muskegon, MI 49441; www.muskegon-mi.gov
Petoskey State Park	90	2475 M-119 Highway, Petoskey MI, 49770; 231-347-2311; www.michigan.org
Pictured Rocks National Lakeshore	114	South shore of Lake Superior in Michigan's Upper Peninsula; www.nps.gov/piro/index.htm
Point Iroquois Lighthouse	106	12942 Lakeshore Drive West, Brimley, MI 49715; 906-437-5272; www.exploringthenorth.com/ptiroquois/iroquois.html
Porcupine Mountains Wilderness State Park	120	33303 Headquarters Road, Ontonagon MI, 49953; 906-885-5275; www.michigan.gov/porkies

Silver Beach Carousel	54	333 Broad Street, St. Joseph, MI 49085; 269-982-8500; www.silverbeachcarousel.com
Silver Lake Sand Dunes and Little Sable Point Lighthouse	80	Dunes chamber of commerce: 2388 Comfort Drive North, Hart, MI 49420; 231-873-2247; www.thinkdunes.com; along Lake Michigan's shoreline between Muskegon and Ludington Lighthouse: 287 Lighthouse Drive North, Mears, MI 49436; www.lighthousefriends.com
Sleeping Bear Dunes National Lakeshore	86	Sleeping Bear Dunes National Lakeshore, Dune Highway South, Empire, MI 49630; 231-326-5134; www.nps.gov/slbe/index.htm
Soo Locks	104	Visitor Center: 312 Portage Avenue West, Sault Ste. Marie, MI 49783; 906-253-9290; www.lre.usace.army.mil
S.S. *Badger*	84	WI: 900 Lakeview Drive South, Manitowoc, WI 54220; MI: 701 Maritime Drive, Ludington, MI 49431; 800-841-4243; www.ssbadger.com
Sugarloaf Mountain	116	6 miles northwest of Marquette, MI along County Road 550; www.co.marquette.mi.us
Tahquamenon Falls	110	41382 M-123 West, Paradise, MI 49768; 906-492-3415; www.michigan.gov/dnr
The Henry Ford and Greenfield Village	46	20900 Oakwood Boulevard, Dearborn, MI 48124; 800.835.5237; www.thehenryford.org
U-M's Matthaei Botanical Gardens and Nichols Arboretum, and the Big House	48	Botanical Gardens: 1800 Dixboro Road North, Ann Arbor, MI 48105; 734-647-7600; www.lsa.umich.edu/mbg/see/NicholsArboretum.asp Big House: 1201 Main Street South, Ann Arbor, MI 48104; 734-647-2583; www.mgoblue.com/facilities/michigan-stadium.html
Windmill Island Gardens and Tulip Time Festival	70	1 Lincoln Avenue, Holland, MI 49423; 616-355-1030; www.cityofholland.com/windmillislandgardens
Zehnder's Holz Brücke Covered Bridge	8	Main Street & Covered Bridge Lane, Frankenmuth, MI 48734; 800-386-8696; www.michigan.org

Photo credits, continued from page 2